Front cover illustration:
Head-on view of the Mil Mi-28 'Havoc', the newest Soviet attack helicopter. The nose dome covers the missile guidance antenna for its eight AT-6 'Spiral' anti-tank missiles, while the chin-mounted electro-optics turret contains the target acquisition sight and laser rangefinder. The inboard pylons carry two UB-20 pods each with eight S-8 unguided missiles, while the turret gun is derived from the 2A42 30mm autocannon originally mounted on the BMP-2 armoured infantry vehicle.

Back cover illustration, top:
Mi-8TB belonging to Transporthubschraubergeschwader 34 'Werner Seelenbinder', photographed at Holzdorf air base in June 1990. The East German unit has 24 'Hips' and normally operates from Brandenburg-Briest, a well-known Luftwaffe base during the Second World War.

Back cover illustration, bottom:
Romanian troops disembarking from an Mi-4 'Hound' with the tactical number 'White 2'.

1. An East German Mi-1 being overhauled. The AI-26V radial engine provides a maximum take-off power of 575hp and is installed vertically in the rear half of the fuselage. The engine is cooled by a ventilator to avoid overheating in the hover. The main rotor is a tapered steel tube spar, while the tail rotor blades are of wood with a plywood and fabric cover. Both rotors are medium green in colour and the tail rotor's warning stripes are in black and white.

BEVERLEY GROUP			
BEL		NOF	
BRD	898	POC	444
DRI	94	SKI	
ELL		SOU	
EVE		STB	
FLA		SWA	
FSP		WIT	
HED		COM S	
HOR		MOB	
LEV		TR2	
LIT		BER	
MAR			

SOVIET
MILITARY
HELICOPTERS

HANS-HEIRI STAPFER

ARMS AND
ARMOUR

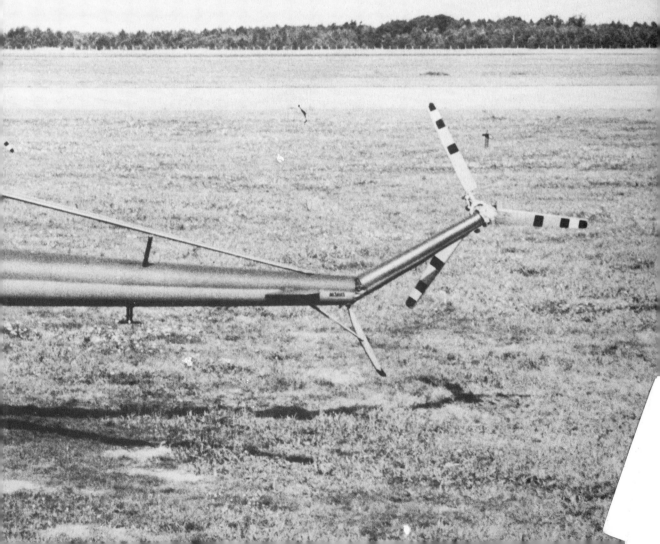

Arms and Armour Press
A Cassell Imprint
Villiers House, 41–47 Strand, London WC2N 5JE.

Distributed in the USA by Sterling Publishing Co. Inc., 387 Park
Avenue South, New York, NY 10016-8810.

Distributed in Australia by Capricorn Link (Australia) Pty. Ltd,
P.O. Box 665, Lane Cove, New South Wales 2066.

British Library Cataloguing in Publication Data
Stapfer, Hans-Heiri
Soviet military helicopters.
1. Union of Soviet Socialist Republics. Military aircraft.
Helicopters.
I. Title
623.7460470947
ISBN 1-85409-110-7

Designed and edited by DAG Publications Ltd. Designed by David
Gibbons; edited by David Dorrell; layout by Anthony A. Evans;
typeset by Ronset Typesetters, Darwen, Lancashire; camerawork by
M&E Reproductions, North Fambridge, Essex; printed and bound in
Great Britain by The Alden Press, Oxford.

2. The first Soviet rotary-wing aircraft to fly was the KASKR-1, named Krasnij Inzhener' ('Red Engineer'). Designed by Nikolai I. Kamov and Nikolai K. Skrzhinsky, it first flew in 1929. Its fuselage was taken from a licence-built Avro 504K biplane trainer and the autogyro was powered by a Gnôme-Rhône engine. [*Robert Gretzyngier*]

3. The TsAGI A-7bis was the first Soviet autogyro to be built in series, although only five machines resulted. The prototype A-7 first flew on 20 September 1934 and was introduced to the public during the Tushino air display in August 1935. The A-7bis saw action in the Second World War with the five aircraft operating from a base near Smolensk and undertaking close reconnaissance and leaflet-dropping missions. [*Robert Gretzyngier*]

INTRODUCTION

The Soviet Union has a long tradition of helicopter construction. Its first rotary-wing aircraft, an autogyro, flew in 1930 and since then there have been some remarkable achievements: the Mi-6, V-12, and Mi-26 have all been the world's largest rotorcraft in their time, and the Mi-24 is believed by many experts to be the world's most potent attack helicopter.

The evolution of rotary-wing aircraft in the USSR has been very different from that in the West and only two manufacturers exist, Kamov and Mil. Each firm specialized in a single type, thereby ensuring standardization and high production numbers. Only a few components – engines, gearboxes, parts of the rotor and tail system – can be interchanged between the Mi-8, Mi-17, Mi-14, and Mi-24.

The Soviet Union is the world's largest and most inhospitable country, and the helicopter has made it possible to open up the otherwise inaccessible areas of Siberia in order to exploit the vast oil and natural gas reserves. Without the 'flying crane' capability offered by the Mi-6, Mi-10, and Mi-26, it is doubtful whether the pipelines could have been completed as quickly as they have been.

Russian designs date back to 1754 when M. Lamonosov built a model of a lifting airscrew, but it was not until the late 1920s that the KASKR-1 autogyro was unveiled by N. I. Kamov and N. K. Skrzhinsky. The first to fly successfully for any period was the TsAGI A-7 autogyro which took to the skies in 1934 and was to see action in a reconnaissance role around Smolensk in the early weeks of Russia's involvement in the Second World War.

More urgent projects led to the downgrading of rotorcraft development during that conflict. Kamov continued his work and other talented designers also entered the field, notably Bratukhin, Mil and Yakovlev. In September 1948 Mil's Mi-1 (NATO code-name 'Hare') became the first successful Soviet helicopter, beating Yakovlev's Yak-100 which had been copied from the American Sikorsky S-51. Kamov's first effort, the Ka-8, was nicknamed the 'Flying Motorcycle', and in September 1949 he produced the Ka-10, retaining

the co-axial contra-rotating rotor system that made the large tail boom and anti-torque tail rotor unnecessary. The first operational type adopting this design was the Ka-15 in 1952, followed soon after by the Ka-18 'Hog' in 1957.

In October 1951 Stalin had requested a larger helicopter and Yakovlev and Mil took up the challenge. The resultant Yak-24, nicknamed 'Flying Boxcar', was a failure, suffering from dangerous vibration and other shortcomings. Its tandem configuration of one rotor at the front and one on the tail was not used again; nor were any further helicopter designs from Yakovlev. Mil's Mi-4 'Hound' was more successful, going into service in April 1952 just seven months after work had begun on the design. The Mi-4 has since seen considerable use as a military and a civil helicopter.

In the mid-1950s the first steps were taken towards designing heavy-payload helicopters able to lift 12,000kg (26,460lb or 11.8 tons). These were needed both to exploit Siberia and to give the air force a battlefield reinforcement capability, carrying in heavy weapons, supplies, etc which no fixed-wing aircraft could do. The result was the Mil Mi-6, a gigantic helicopter which was the first Russian type to use turbines rather than piston engines as its powerplant. Despite its size and weight, the Mi-6 became the first helicopter to exceed the 300km/h speed barrier when, on 21 September 1961, N. Liochin achieved 320km/h.

A rival design was the Kamov Ka-22 'Hoop', which only appeared in public once at the Tushino air display in 1961. It is the only Kamov design not to feature co-axial contra-rotating rotors, having an Ivchenko AI-20V propeller turbine mounted at each end of a tapered wing. A more successful Kamov was the Ka-25 'Hormone', a ship-borne anti-submarine helicopter which went through several variants: the 'Hormone-B' with special electronics providing over-the-horizon target acquisition capabilities, and the 'Hormone-C' utility and search/rescue helicopter. The Ka-25 became operational in 1966 and was the main ship-based naval helicopter of the 1960s and '70s. It was replaced in the early 1980s by the Ka-32 'Helix', powered by two Isotov Tv-3-117 engines, with improved ASW equipment and a greater range.

Meanwhile, the Mil design bureau had begun to appreciate the advantages offered by the gas turbine: the powerplant weighed less than a piston engine, and it only required cheap jet kerosene rather than expensive high-octane fuel. The Mil team then set about developing a successor to the 'Hare' and 'Hound'. In 1961 they flew the prototype Mi-2 'Hoplite' powered by two Isotov GTD-350 engines. In 1965 production of the Mi-2 began at WSK-Swidnik in Poland and as late as the 1980s the 'Hoplite' remained the standard Warsaw Pact liaison and medevac helicopter. The 'Hound's' successor is the Mi-8 'Hip' which, at 28 people, has double the 'Hound's capacity but only a slightly larger airframe. The 'Hip' is powered by two Isotov TV-2-117s, and was the first attack helicopter in the Soviet inventory. Numerically it remains the backbone of the Soviet transport regiments, but its firepower means that the Mi-8TB can carry four UB-32 pods, and the Mi-8TBK six UB-32 pods plus anti-tank missiles.

The Ka-26 'Hoodlum' was designed for agricultural work and, powered by two Vedeneyev M-14 V-26 nine-cylinder radial engines, first flew in 1964. It has only been used in a military capacity by Hungary, who employed it as a scout and liaison helicopter until recently. In October 1988 the Ka-26 was superseded by the single-turboshaft-engined Ka-126 developed at the Kamov plant in Uchta. Early in 1990 mass production of the Ka-126 began at Brasov in Romania, and there are plans to convert many of the old Ka-26s to turbine power.

The best-known Soviet helicopter, the Mil Mi-24 'Hind', first flew in 1969. The USSR's first dedicated gunship, it also had a retractable undercarriage which enabled the 'Hind' to surpass the 320km/h limit. It has been through numerous variants: the 'Hind-A' had a vulnerable 'greenhouse' cockpit which was eliminated in the 'Hind-D', and the designation 'Hind-E' was given to machines fitted with AT-6 'Spiral' missiles. However, it was the war in Afghanistan that had the greatest effect on the 'Hind's development; its altitude performance has been improved remarkably, and the modern war environment led to the fitting of an infra-red counter-measures jammer pod as well as chaff/flare dispensers to combat the highly effective

4. The Mil Mi-1 was the Soviet Union's first mass-produced helicopter. It beat the Yakovlev Yak-100, which was in fact a copy of the American Sikorsky S-51. The Mi-1 had a better performance; it had a lower empty weight but a greater gross weight than the Yak-100. The Mi-1 flew for the first time in 1948, some nine months after the Mil design bureau had been established in December 1947.

4

US Stinger ground-to-air missiles. The 'Hind's' fire-power has also been increased with the creation of the 'Hind-F', a version that has had its four-barrel 12.7mm gun replaced by a GSh 23mm twin-barrel cannon fitted on the starboard side. The 'Hind-F' has not been exported outside the USSR.

The Mi-14 'Haze' is a specially designed naval helicopter which exists in three variants: Mi-14PL for anti-submarine warfare, Mi-14BT for mine-detection and mine-countermeasures, and Mi-14PS for search and rescue. It was brought into service in the 1970s to replace the ageing Mi-4MA. The Mi-8 too has its replacement in the shape of the Mi-17 'Hip-H', which is basically an improved and slightly larger Mi-8. The engine is a TV-3-117MT and the tail rotor has been moved from starboard to port. The Mi-17 is in civil use with Aeroflot as well as in military service.

The largest Soviet helicopter is the Mi-26 'Halo', which can carry a payload of 20,000kg (nearly 20 tons). Its underslung load capability is the same as can be carried in the cargo compartment. It first flew in 1977 and has a maximum gross weight of 56,000kg!

The development of heavy cargo helicopters such as the Mi-26 and Mi-6 has placed the Soviet Union at the forefront of this aspect of technology, but the appearance at the 1989 Paris Air Show of the Mi-28 'Havoc' now suggests that the Russians may well lead the world in gunship design too.

The highly sophisticated 'Havoc' first flew in November 1982. A great deal of Afghanistan experience went into its design: the cockpit is heavily armoured and can survive crashes at an impact of 15m/second; the rotor head is made of titanium and the blades are composites; it has a flexible 23mm cannon, sixteen AT-6 'Spirals' on its pylons and two pods each carrying twenty 105mm missiles. The 'Havoc' does not carry troops but its potential is plain to see; full production is planned for 1991.

These designs augur well for the future and consolidate the Soviet Union's position as a leading manufacturer of the world's helicopters.

5. 'Black HK-3', an SM-1 'Hare', the first type of helicopter in Finnish Air Force service. The type was Polish-built; the only Soviet-built machine was donated to Finland by Nikita Krushchev on the occasion of Finnish President Urho Kekkonen's 60th birthday. The neutral Finns operated the 'Hare' between 1960 and 1968. [Hannu Valtonen]

6. 'Red 31', an Mi-1M of the Magyar Légierö (Hungarian Air Force) at Budaörs airfield near Budapest. The Mi-1 was used by the Hungarians for liaison and medevac before being replaced by the Ka-26 'Hoodlum'. The avionics of the Mi-1 included an ARK-5 radio compass, GIK-1 gyrocompass, and an RV-2 radio altimeter. The Mi-1 was also used by the Hungarian Police. [Laszlo Javor]

7. In 1943 Nikolai I. Kamov was the first Russian to begin work on a helicopter with a co-axial contra-rotating twin rotor system. The resultant Ka-8 'Hat' first flew in 1948, the same time as the Mi-1 'Hare' flew for the first time. The Ka-8 interested the Soviet Navy and could even carry two people, albeit under rather windy flight conditions. This was acceptable in summer, but in the bitterly cold Soviet winter conditions it was not recommended. [*Robert Gretzyngier*]

8. A refined Ka-8, designated Ka-8M, demonstrates its ability to land on a ZIL-150 four-and-a-half truck.

The Ka-8M had a new twin rudder control system, a service ceiling of 2,500 metres and a top speed of 116km/h. [*Robert Gretzyngier*]

9. In 1952 the Kamov Ka-15 'Hen' made its first flight. Powered by a 255hp Ivchenko AI-14V engine, it had a top speed of 150 km/h and could climb to an altitude of 3,000 metres. The two antennas with the reversed 'T' shape are for the RV-2 radio altimeter. This example belongs to the Soviet Navy and is painted medium grey overall. [*Robert Gretzyngier*]

10. The Aeroflot Kamov Ka-15M, seen here, was used for training, passenger and mail transport, and for reconnaissance flights operating from ice-breakers. It differed from the Ka-15 in a number of details: a central fin was added to the tail and a small antenna was placed behind the rear RV-2 radio altimeter antenna. [*Robert Gretzyngier*]

11. The Ka-18 'Hog' was a stretched version of the Ka-15 and first flew in 1957. It could carry four people in two rows and differed from the Ka-15 in having an enlarged nose and larger tail fins. [*Robert Gretzyngier*]

12. The Mi-4 'Hound' was developed, quite remarkably, in just seven months. It was powered by a Shvetsov ASh-82V radial engine – powerplant of the famous Lavochkin fighters in the Second World War. The Mi-4 has served for more than three decades in the Soviet Union's and WarPac's inventories.

13. The 'Hound' prototype, V-4, was powered by a Shvetsov ASh-62IR engine, the standard powerplant for the Antonov An-2 'Colt' biplane. However, it developed only 1,000hp and this was considered insufficient for the Mi-4, which lost a great deal of energy via gearbox and tail rotor transmission. The problem was solved with the more powerful ASh-82V engine which, as seen here, created large exhaust fumes. A fire extinguisher was always placed close to hand when starting.

14. 'White D-56', an Mi-4A of the Czech Air Force carrying a rather unusual tactical marking, which is believed to be applied only during an exercise. This particular 'Hound' has just unloaded a GAZ-69 vehicle and a 57mm anti-tank cannon. The 'Hound' has a payload of 1,700kg, but this figure drops dramatically on hot and dry summer days because of the reduction in engine power.

15

15. 'Black HR-3', a Finnish Air Force Mi-4A, with a Messerschmitt Bf 109F-4 (Werk Nr 7108) as its underslung load. This particular Bf 109F was built in 1941 by the Messerschmitt factory at Wiener-Neustadt near Vienna, Austria. It has the markings 'NE+ML' and probably belonged to the JG 5 'Eismeerjäger'.

16. Polish soldiers in winter uniform board an Mi-4 during an exercise; the Mi-4 can carry up to sixteen fully armed troops. The single digit tactical number 'White 2' indicates that this took place early in the Mi-4's service with the Polish Air Force. On later types, the fatigue life of the rotor blades was raised from 100 hours to 1,500 hours, while a heavy reduction gearbox reduced the engine's rpm on the rotor from 2,400 to 178.

17. Frogmen leaving an East German Mi-4A, 'White 574', during a parade of the East German Navy at Rostock to celebrate the 20th anniversary of the foundation of the German Democratic Republic (9 October 1969). These oversized white tactical numbers, with small black outlines, were only carried for a short period in the late 1960s.

18. The first Mi-4s were received by the German Democratic Republic in 1957 and this Mi-4A, 'Black 535', carries the old East German insignia without the yellow hammer and sickle symbol in the centre. The 'Hound' was the first helicopter in the inventory of the East German Air Force. The Mi-4As were allocated to Transporthubschraubergeschwader 34 'Werner Seelenbinder' with which they served until withdrawn from operations in August 1978. The very

last flight was in 1980 when Lt-Col Gottfried Tübel ferried the last Mi-4A from East Germany to the Hungarian Army Museum in Budapest.

19. East German Mi4-As were often involved in medevac flights. 'Black 655' is collecting a seriously ill person at Marx-Engels Platz in East Berlin to fly him to a hospital at Halle in the south of the republic. The Mi-4 can carry up to eight stretchers. From 1962 onwards the Mi-4 was assigned to Fighter Regiment 9 'Heinrich Rau', based at Peenemünde on the Baltic, where its duty was air-sea rescue. For this task it received a jettisonable liferaft and additional radio equipment.

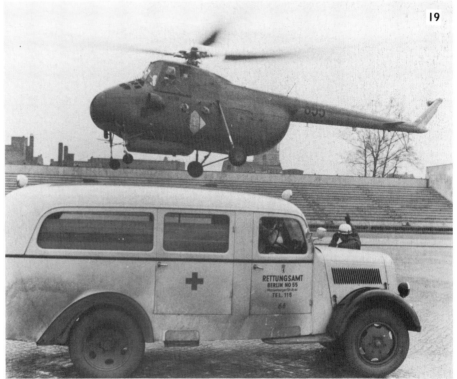

20. An Mi-4A at Budaörs airfield carrying revolutionary markings of a red-white-and-green rectangle during the Hungarian uprising of 1956. Few such aircraft took to the skies and the rising was crushed by the Russians. In attempting to regain control of the airfields, at least three Russian Mi-4s carrying assault troops were shot down by the Hungarians. [*George Punka*]

21. This Mi-4A is operated by East Germany's Interflug-Spezialflug. It is a former air force 'Hound' with the national markings replaced by the civil registration DM-SPF. As is usual when the Mi-4 is used in the flying crane role, the two clamshell doors as well the portside entrance doors have been removed to reduce weight and increase the payload. If used as a crane, the pilot flies while the co-pilot checks the instruments and looks for hindrances on either side of the helicopter. At the same time, the flight engineer gets in the ventral gondola to keep an eye on the underslung cargo.

22. The Mi-4 'Hound-C' is used for relaying radio transmissions and plays a vital liaison role between low-flying fighter aircraft when on tactical operations and the home base. It has additional antennas fitted under the fuselage and tail boom.

23. On the passenger variant of the Mi-4, the Mi-4P, the four round cabin windows were replaced by three square windows. The nose and main wheels were enclosed in spats, while the gondola below the fuselage was deleted. The 'Hound' could carry, depending on the variant, ten to sixteen passengers. The Mi-4L was a de-luxe version with only six passengers, a chair and a small galley. Some Mi-4s were also given to WarPac air forces to serve as VIP transports. [*Hannu Valtonen*]

22

23

24. An Mi-4MA 'Hound-B' with magnetic anomaly detection (MAD) gear fully deployed. This type has a shorter gondola without a TKB-481 gun, and a type RBP-4G search radar under the nose. Behind the gondola are two large bomb bay doors, while on the clamshell doors below the MAD gear housing is a hatch for a large liferaft.

25. A Polish Navy Mi-4MA 'Hound-B' anti-submarine helicopter takes off from its base. This type always works in pairs: one is the search helicopter which locates the target with the help of sonobuoys and marks its position with green dye, while the other carries the charges to destroy the submarine. The cargo compartment can hold up to four 250kg or six 100kg anti-submarine bombs.

26. The Yak-24 'Horse' was the last helicopter design of Alexander Yakovlev. It first flew in July 1952 and was powered by two ASh-82V engines located in the front and rear of the fuselage. The Yak-24 could carry 37 to 40 fully equipped infantrymen and due its distinctive appearance was nicknamed 'Flying Boxcar'. It was the sole Soviet helicopter of tandem rotor layout. This particular machine was used to replace the roof beams of Katherine's Palace, Leningrad, in 1959. [*Martin Bowman*]

27. Work began on the design of the Mi-6 'Hook' in 1954, and the prototype V-6 Shestjorka first flew on 5 June 1957, powered by two 4,635shp TV-2BM turbines. The Mi-6 was the first Soviet helicopter with turboshaft engines, instead of the piston engines used on the Mi-1 and Mi-4. It was built after the Soviet Government had issued a strange specification for a helicopter whose take-off weight was to be seven times greater than that of the Mi-4! The V-6, seen here, had several features that did not appear on the production 'Hook': the main wheel spats, no auxiliary fuel tank provision and smaller windows in the radio operator's compartment. [*Dr Volker Koos*]

28. 'Red 02', an Mi-6T which is part of the GSFG (Group Soviet Forces Germany) undergoing engine maintenance. Part of the engine covering can be used as a working platform for the ground crew. Each Soloviev D-25V engine is rated at 5,500shp and weighs 1,325kg. The huge R-7 gearbox alone weighs 3,200kg and these three items combined have a greater weight than one empty Mi-4 'Hound' or two Mi-2 'Hoplites'.

29

30

29. 'Red 54', an Mi-6T (serial number 85640048), lands on a field to unload troops and vehicles. This will take no more than 40 seconds, but the navigator mans a defensive TKB-481 gun if needed. The Mi-6 can carry 65 fully equipped soldiers and its large cargo hold can accommodate heavy weapons such as the ASU-57 self-propelled assault gun or light AA guns.

30. An Mi-6A of the Polish commercial operator Instal is refuelled by a Soviet Ural 375 fuel truck. The size of the truck lends scale to the large dimensions of the Mi-6 'Hook', which has an internal fuel capacity of 8,150 litres divided among eleven fuel tanks. In addition, a 2,800-litre tank can be fitted on each side of the fuselage. The average fuel consump- tion of an Mi-6 in flight is about 2,400 litres per hour and the most fuel-efficient speed is 170km/h.

31. The Ka-22 'Hoop' is the largest Kamov helicopter to have been built and is the only one from this design bureau to have two contra- rotating rotors placed on the end of a tapered stub wing. It is powered by two Ivchenko AI-20V propeller turbines which each drive a rotor as well as a conven- tional four-bladed propeller for fast forward flight. Design work began in 1954 and the prototype flew for the first time on 17 June 1959. The 'Hoop' emerged from the same design com- petition as the Mi-6 but, given the 'Hook's superior- ity, the Ka-22 never entered production. [*Robert Gretzyngier*]

32. 'Yellow 22'', an early Yak-24 'Horse', nicknamed 'Flying Boxcar'. Built in 1955, the 'Horse' suffered from structural vibration in flight and as a result production was terminated after one hundred had been built.

For its time it was an advanced design, with twin rotor configuration and two ASh-82V engines.

33. Final assembly of an Mi-2 'Hoplite' at the PZL factory at Swidnik, near Lublin in Poland. The Mi-2 on the left is a civil variant, while that on the right has the standard camouflage for the early period: dark green on upper surfaces and light blue on the lower surfaces. The mechanic at the front is working on the accumulator compartment and the black boxes are two acid storage batteries waiting to be installed. [*PZL Swidnik*]

34. Mi-2 production line at Swidnik in Poland. Developed by the Mil design bureau in the USSR, the first of only two prototypes flew in late 1961 (registration SSSR-06180). After successful trials and government acceptance, the project was transferred to Poland, where the first Mi-2 flew in November 1965 and mass produc-tion began the following year. This gave the Russians more capacity for other types, such as the Mi-6 and Mi-8. The Poles' annual output is now nearly 300 helicopters, most of which are exported to the Soviet Union. All WarPac countries are equipped with this light helicopter and the 'Hoplite has been exported to Bul-garia, North Korea, Czecho-slovakia, East Germany, Hungary, Indonesia, Iraq, Libya, Syria, USA, USSR and Yugoslavia. [*PZL Swidnik*]

35. A formation of three Polish Air Force Mi-2s – 'White 603', 'White 285' and 'White 199'. All three carry the white-and-red band on the tail boom which identi-fies them as belonging to the one hundred or more cur-rently serving with the Polish Air Force or Navy. These helicopters are from an early production batch, identifiable by the dark green camouflage which was later exchanged for a two- or even three-tone camouflage.

ASCC REPORTING NAMES

The reporting names are not part of Soviet aircraft designations but a means adopted by NATO's Air Standards Co-ordinating Committee (ASCC) to allow rapid radio identification and reporting of Soviet aircraft types. The names are all designed to sound different so that they will not be confused even under conditions of poor radio reception.

ASCC Reporting Name	Soviet Designation	ASCC Reporting Name	Soviet Designation
'Halo'	Mi-26	'Hip-C'	Mi-8TB with four weapon pylons as assault version
'Hare'	Mi-1		
'Harke-A'	Mi-10 (long-leg undercarriage)	'Hip-D'*	Mi-9 for airborne communications role
'Harke-B'	Mi-10K (short-leg undercarriage)		
'Harp'	Ka-20 (forerunner of Ka-25 'Hormone')	'Hip-E'	Mi-8TBK with 12.7mm gun and six weapon pylons
'Hat'	Ka-8	'Hip-F'	Mi-8TBK for export
'Havoc'	Mi-28	'Hip-G'*	Mi-9 airborne communications version
'Haze-A'	Mi-14PL, anti-submarine variant		
'Haze-B'	Mi-14BT, mine counter-measures variant	'Hip-H'	Mi-17
'Helix-A'	Ka-32, basic anti-submarine variant	'Hip-J'	ECM/communications jamming variant
'Helix-B'	Ka-32, infantry assault transport variant	'Hip-K'	Mi-8 for communications jamming ECM version
'Helix-C'	Ka-32, SAR and plane guard variant	'Hog'	Ka-18
'Hen'	Ka-15	'Homer'	V-12 (not mass-produced, therefore no 'Mi' prefix)
'Hind-A'	Mi-24A, first production variant with 'greenhouse' cockpit	'Hoodlum-A'	Kamov Ka-26
'Hind-B'	V-24, prototype of the 'Hind-A'	'Hoodlum-B'	Kamov Ka-126
'Hind-C'	Mi-24A, training variant without nose gun and AT-2 missile rails	'Hook'	Mi-6
		'Hoop'	Ka-22
'Hind-D'	Mi-24D, improved variant with tandem cockpit and new nose	'Hoplite'	Mi-2
		'Hormone-A'	Ka-25 anti-submarine version
'Hind-E'	Mi-24V, provision for AT-6 'Spiral' missiles on end plates	'Hormone-B'	Ka-25 over-the-horizon target acquisition version
'Hind-F'	Mi-24 P, GSh-23L cannon on starboard side instead of 12.7mm gun	'Hormone-C'	Ka-25 SAR and utility variant
		'Horse'	Yak-24
'Hind-G'	ECM variant without AT-6 missile rails and guidance/LLTV pods	'Hound-A'	Mi-4A military transport
		'Hound-B'	Mi-4MA anti-submarine version with large radome on nose
'Hip-A'	V-8 prototype with single 2,700shp Soloviev engine	'Hound-C'	Mi-4A radio relaying variant with additional antennas
'Hip-B'	V-8 prototype with two TV-2-117 engines		

*The airborne communications version of the Mi-8 is generally called Mi-9 in Soviet military use.

CAMOUFLAGE AND MARKINGS

Ka-25: Most Ka-25 'Hormone' helicopters are painted light grey overall with national markings applied on the fin and the under surfaces of the fuselage.

Ka-26: The Ka-26 'Hoodlum' in civil use is seen in many varied colour schemes. Military Ka-26s in Hungary are olive drab on the upper and light blue on the lower surfaces. National markings are applied on both sides of the fuselage and on the under surfaces. The red tactical number is outlined in white.

Ka-32: The Ka-32 'Helix' is generally light grey overall with national markings applied on the fin and the under surface of the fuselage. SAR Ka-32s are painted in white and yellow.

Yak-24: The Yak-24 'Horse' in military service is dark green on the upper and light blue on the under surfaces. National markings are applied only on the tail of the fuselage on both sides. The tactical number is mainly large in the front and small on top of the tail.

Mi-1: Most Mi-1s in military service are dark green on the upper and light blue on the lower surfaces. The tactical number is applied on the tail boom and the national marking is applied mainly on the tail boom. Rotor blades are in medium grey.

Mi-2: Early Mi-2s were painted in dark green on the upper surfaces and light blue on the lower surfaces. By now most 'Hoplites' carry a two-tone camouflage of either light green/medium green, olive drab/earth brown or sand-yellow/olive drab. Some Mi-2s are seen with three-tone camouflage of olive drab/sand-yellow/light grey. Rotor blades are in medium grey with silver leading edges for the de-icing system.

Mi-4: Early Mi-4s were painted dark green (upper) and light blue (lower surfaces). Some Mi-4s were painted in light green/olive drab. Polish Mi-4s also had earth brown/light grey/olive drab camouflage and East German 'Hounds' had an olive drab/earth brown camouflage. National markings were applied on both sides of the rear fuselage on the undersurfaces. The tactical number appeared mainly on the tail boom, or on the front of the fuselage.

Mi-6: The Mi-6 'Hook' was painted light grey overall. The tactical number was applied mainly in red and had three digits. Early Mi-6s also had yellow two-digit numbers. The serial number was applied in black on the port side of the tail boom only. Wheel coverings were mainly in bright dark green. Main and tail rotors were in medium grey with silver leading edges. Polish Mi-6s are dark green on the upper and light blue on the lower surfaces.

Mi-8: Early Mi-8s were painted in dark green with light blue undersurfaces. This was followed by a light grey/olive drab camouflage. Some Mi-8s were also painted in olive drab/light grey/dark brown or olive drab/light grey/sand-yellow. East German and Hungarian Mi-8s are camouflaged in olive drab/earth brown. The inside of the engine covering and the cockpit is mainly light grey; in some 'Hips' also light blue. The rotor is medium grey with silver leading edges. National markings are applied on the rear of the fuselage and the under surfaces. Soviet Mi-8s mainly have the tactical number applied on the fuselage, while most WarPac countries have them on the tail boom.

Mi-14: Most Mi-14 'Hazes' have light grey upper and light blue under surfaces. Part of the area behind the exhaust stubs is in black. The tactical number is applied mainly on the fuselage. National markings are painted on the under surfaces and both sides of the fuselage. East German Mi-14s have a dark blue/light blue camouflage and black tactical numbers on the tail boom. Polish Mi-14PS SAR helicopters have a red flash through the fuselage and a red Samaritan cross painted against a white circle. Rotor blades are medium grey with silver leading edges. Undercarriage and wheel covers are generally in glossy light grey. The inside of the cockpit is also mainly painted in light grey.

Mi-17: The 'Hip-H' normally has light grey/olive drab upper surfaces and light blue under surfaces. Some Mi-17s in service are painted olive drab/light grey/sand-yellow or olive drab/light grey/earth brown. Mi-17s in Afghanistan sometimes have a tan/olive drab camouflage.

Mi-24: Early Mi-24 'Hind-As' were camouflaged in light grey and olive drab. Others were camouflaged in light brown/earth brown. The early Mi-24 'Hind-Ds' were also seen in light grey/olive drab. Standard for the Mi-24 'Hind-D' and Mi-24 'Hind-E' was a camouflage of light green/olive drab. Mi-24s operated in the Asian part of the Soviet Union, as well as in Afghanistan, were camouflaged in tan and olive drab. On all the Mi-24 variants the under surfaces are light blue. Soviet Mi-24 'Hind-D/Hind-E' carry the national marking on the rear half of the fuselage and on the under surfaces. The tactical number is applied either on the tail boom or the first half of the fuselage. Rotor blades are painted medium grey with silver leading edges.

Mi-26: Military Mi-26s mainly carry a three-tone camouflage of olive drab/light grey/earth brown. Under surfaces are light blue. Vortex/debris guards are sometimes silver. The tactical number is mainly of two digits in yellow outlined in black.

National markings are painted on the rear half of the fuselage and on the under surfaces.

Mi-28: Three-tone camouflage of olive drab/medium green/earth brown on the upper surfaces and light blue on the under surfaces. The cockpit interior is chromate green. Rotor blades are medium grey with silver leading edges.

36. A battery check and engine change on a light-green/olive-drab Mi-2, 'White 2642'. The heavy (140kg) GTD-3500 engine can be removed easily with the help of a crane fitted to the rotor head once the rotor blade itself has been removed. This ensures a proper engine change even under the worst conditions, since all the tools can be carried in the helicopter. The large access hatches in the front enable important items to be maintained and checked easily. This particular 'Hoplite' is fitted with a 23mm cannon on the port side.

36

SPECIFICATIONS

Type	KASKR-1	TsAGI A-7bis	Ka-8 'Hat'	Ka-25 'Hormone'	Ka-26 'Hoodlum'	Ka-32 'Helix'	Yak-24 'Horse'
ASCC name	–						
Rotor diameter	12.00m	15.18m	6.12m	15.77m	13.03m	15.90m	21.00m
Fuselage length	9.00m	8.39m	3.90m	9.75m	7.75m	11.30m	21.34m
Height	3.80m	3.74m	2.50m	5.37m	4.05m	5.40m	6.50m
Empty weight	600kg	1,300kg	234kg	4,765kg	1,950kg	5,250kg	10,607kg
Max. gross weight	700kg	2,000kg	375kg	7,485kg	3,250kg	12,600kg	16,000kg
Max. speed	60km/h	210km/h	116km/h	210km/h	169km/h	250km/h	175km/h
Range	–	–	193km	400km	400km	800km	265km
Ceiling	40m	4,800m	2,500m	3,500m	3,000m	5,000m	4,200m
Engine	Gnome-Rhone (110hp)	M-22 (430hp)	AI-4V (55hp)	GTD-3F (900shp)	M-14V-26 (325shp)	TV-3-117 (2,225shp)	ASh-82V (1,700hp)
First flight	1929	1934	1947	1960	1965	1978	1952

Type	Mi-1 'Hare'	Mi-2 'Hoplite'	Mi-4 'Hound'	Mi-6A 'Hook'	Mi-8TB 'Hip-C'	Mi-17 'Hip-H'	Mi-24D 'Hind-D'	Mi-26 'Halo'	Mi-28 'Havoc'
ASCC name									
Rotor diameter	14.35m	14.56m	21.10m	35.00m	21.29m	21.29m	17.00m	32.00m	17.20m
Fuselage length	12.10m	11.94m	16.79m	33.18m	18.31m	18.42m	16.80m	33.73m	16.85
Height	3.30m	3.75m	4.40m	9.86m	5.60m	5.60m	5.70m	8.06m	3.84m
Empty weight	1,863kg	2,372kg	4,900kg	27,240kg	7,500kg	7,100kg	8,400kg	28,200kg	6,500kg
Max. gross weight	2,550kg	3,700kg	7,550kg	42,500kg	12,000kg	13,000kg	11,000kg	56,000kg	10,400kg
Max. speed	204km/h	210km/h	210km/h	300km/h	230km/h	250km/h	320km/h	295km/h	300km/h
Range	370km	170km	440km	1,050km	450km	465km	300km	800km	240km
Ceiling	3,000m	4,000m	5,500m	4,500m	4,500m	3,600m	4,500m	4,500	4,500m
Engine	AI-26V (575hp)	GTD-350 (400hp)	ASh-82V (1,700hp)	D-25V (5,500shp)	TV-2-117A (1,500shp)	TV-3-117MT (1,900shp)	TV-3-117A (2,200shp)	D-136 (11,400shp)	TV-3-117V (2,200shp)
First flight	1948	1961	1952	1957	1961	1979	1969	1977	1982

National Marking: The Soviet red star is always in white with a small red outline. Initially the national marking was carried only on the rear half of the fuselage, but by now the national marking on Soviet aircraft is also painted on the under surfaces.

Tactical Number: The tactical number – usually of two digits in yellow, red or white – is carried mainly on the front half of the fuselage. White tactical numbers are generally (but not always) outlined in black.

Weapons: UB-16-57U and UB-32 pods are mainly silver overall. In a few cases the UB-32 can be light blue. The new pod for the 105mm unguided missile is mainly silver with chromate green end plates. The UPK-23 gun pod is in silver. Bombs are without exception dark grey. The gun barrels are gun metal.

37

37. Six Polish Air Force Mi-2s take off for a mission, each with the 238-litre fuel tank on the side. The 'Hoplite' performs a variety of duties: some are assigned to assault regiments for liaison and scout work; others are used in the medevac role with two stretchers located on the starboard side of the fuselage. The two GTD-3500 engines each have a take-off rating of 400shp, which can be maintained for a maximum of 6 minutes; normal cruise rating is 285shp.

A. Mi-6T, tactical number 'Red 79', is of a type that was for long the only heavy-lift helicopter in Warsaw Pact (WarPac) use. It was the first Soviet helicopter with gas turbines and the first in the world to exceed 300km/h. Today it is widely used as a transport helicopter.

B. An Mi-2 'Hoplite' about to take off. It is used for liaison, scout and rescue missions, and although developed in the Soviet Union it is produced exclusively by WSK-Swidnik in Poland.

C. A Hungarian Air Force Mi-8TB 'Hip-C' after touching down at Budaörs airfield. The camouflage scheme is unique in WarPac.

A▲

B▲   C▼

▲D

▲E ▼F

D. A Kamov Ka-29TB attack helicopter, an amphibious variant of the Ka-27 with redesigned nose and a radar guidance pod underneath. It has two UB-20 pods, each of which can carry twenty S-8 80mm unguided rockets with 4kg warheads and used for attacking lightly armoured vehicles.

E. This Mi-24 'Hind-D', seen at Budaörs in June 1988, was one of the first examples the Hungarians received. The 'Hind' is perhaps the most famous of all Soviet helicopters. This particular example is formidably armed. It is fitted with a 'Natasha Device' whose sensors are visible on either side of the nose. This sophisticated ground-to-air missile warning system provides the pilot with the angle of attack as well as identifying the type of missile en route. Its name derives from the fact that information is given by a computerized female voice.

F. Mi-1M 'Red 03' of the Voluntary Society for Assistance to the Army, Air Force, and Navy – better known by its Russian acronym DOSAAF. It has all-metal blades, improved sound-

proofing, instrumentation, and hydraulic controls, plus electrical trim. The housing for the precision low-speed indicator is visible on the tail, while the DOSAAF insignia can be seen in white on the nose. About 250 'Hares' have been exported to the USSR from Poland,

where its designation is SM-1Wb.

G. The spacious interior of the Mi-6T. The cargo compartment is 2.4m high, 2.7m wide, and 11.7m long and can accommodate a maximum payload of 12,000kg. The seats can be folded up

to create more space, and the squared plating can be removed if the cabin hoist is used.

H. The Fuerza Aerea del Peru (Peruvian Air Force) is the sole South American operator of the Mi-6T and operates eight examples.

G▲ 'FAP 682' is seen taking off from Lima's Collique airport in September 1987. Peru's national marking is a red-white-red roundel. Each rotor blade of the Mi-6T weighs 703kg and produces a strong downblast. [*Javier Goto*]

H▼

▲ I

▲ J   ▼ K

I. An Mi-6T belonging to the Peruvian Air Force's Grupo Aerea 3, whose emblem is painted on the nose. All the Grupo's Mi-6s are camouflaged in light and earth brown with light grey undersurfaces, and have black anti-glare panels. The pilot's door has additional armour plating. Most Peruvian Mi-6s have not had stub wings fitted. [*Javier Goto*]

J. After the fall of the Berlin Wall in November 1989, East Germany's Transporthub-schraubergeschwader 34 'Werner Seelenbinder' be-gan to repaint some of its Mi-8s with an orange patch and the letters 'SAR' (for Search and Rescue). These machines were used to attend motorway accidents caused by the vast increase in road traffic between the two Germanies.

K. Several Mi-6Ts are armed with a 12.7mm TKB-481 machine-gun, manually op-erated by the navigator who has a splendid view from his position in the nose. Access to the gun and its ammuni-tion supply is via doors under the fuselage. The chrome-nickel IFF antenna on top of the nose has a permanent protective cover-ing of plastic.

▼ L

L. The 'Hip' is in widespread use with the Yugoslav Air Force and more than 120 have been bought from the USSR. 'White 264' is an Mi-8T, an early variant with dark green camouflage on its upper surfaces. Indeed, the age of the fleet means that it is now coming to the end of its service life as the principal Yugoslav transport helicopter.

M▲ N▼

M. The People's Republic of China operates about forty Mi-8s of various types. There are two passenger versions, the Mi-8P with twenty-eight seats, and the Mi-8S with eleven. This Mi-8P, serial 50450, is about to touch down. Its enlarged side tanks are clearly visible, as is the national marking outlined in yellow.

N. 'Red 836', an early Mi-8TB with the chrome-nickel IFF antenna fitted to the top of the canopy. This 'Hip-C' has a protective fence fitted to the outrigger as protection for parachutists when jumping. Normally when the Mi-8 is used for jumping, the clamshell doors are removed and the parachutists make their exit from the rear.

O. Hungarian paratroops relaxing by their Mi-8TB, 'Red

936'. This early variant lacks a low-speed precision indicator. At the time of writing, more than 8,000 Mi-8s have been built, making it the most numerous Soviet helicopter. About 10 per cent of them have been exported to Hungary and other countries.

O▼

▲P

▲Q

P. A Soviet Mi-17 'Hip-H' at Mosnov-Ostrava air base in Czechoslovakia. It has a chaff/flare dispenser fitted to the tail – a legacy of Afghanistan.

Q. Mi-8TB 'Black 928' of the East German Air Force has a camouflage of olive drab/light grey on the upper and light blue on the lower surfaces. The first GDR unit to receive the Mi-8 was the Transporthubschrau-bergeschwader 34 'Werner Seelenbinder' based at Brandenburg-Briest, closely followed by the assaut regiment Kampfhubschrau-bergeschwader 57 'Adolf von Lützow' at Basephol. A third unit now has the Mi-8 too, KHG 67 'Ferdinand von Schill' at Cottbus, as well as several others assigned to the training unit 'Lambert Horn'.

▲R ▼S

R. A Ka-26 being overhauled in 1988 at Budaörs, Hungary, having completed 1,500 flying hours. The rotor blades and the engine cover-ing have been removed, and much of the cockpit equip-ment has been stripped. The engine is a Vedeneyev M-14V-26 nine-cylinder radial weighing 254kg, double the weight of the Mi-2's GTD-350 turboshaft engine.

T ▲

S. Two Hungarian Ka-26s in a striking yellow colour scheme used when undertaking spraying missions. The nimble 'Hoodlum' can spray relatively short fields and carries a chemical load of 900kg.

T. Three well-known Mil designs lined up together: the nose in the foreground belongs to an Mi-6; in the centre is a flying-crane Mi-10, while in the background is an Mi-8.

U. 'Red 574', an Mi-24D from Hungary, photographed after it had been overhauled and refurbished. It has the latest defensive measures fitted: 'Natasha Device', infra-red suppression boxes, IRCM jammers, short exhaust stubs, and chaff/flare dispensers. [*Gabor Szekeres*]

V. A vehicle being unloaded from a Romanian Air Force Mi-4 'Hound', the first large transport helicopter that service possessed. The national marking seen here was introduced in 1949, replacing the red-yellow-blue roundel of the war years – which has since returned.

U ▲ **V** ▼

▲ W

▲ X   ▼ Y

W. The Mi-28 'Havoc' was designed to incorporate vital lessons learned from Afghanistan. It flew for the first time in November 1982. This photograph was taken during the Paris Air Show at Le Bourget and shows a development prototype powered by two Izotov TV-3-117 engines. Its stub wing and outboard wing pylons enable it to carry sixteen AT-6 'Spiral' missiles; a chin-mounted flexible 23mm cannon is also fitted.

X. Rear view of the 'Havoc' at Paris showing the new exhaust shrouds on the third prototype which draw in outside air, mix it with the exhaust gases and then deflect it downwards. The first two machines had these shrouds mounted further inboard to duct the exhaust upwards, just as on the Mi-24. [Simon Watson]

Y. Close-up of the 'Havoc's' nose and the dome which covers the missile guidance antenna. The chin-mounted electro-optics turret contains the target acquisition sight and the laser rangefinder. On either side there are housings for the pilot's fixed thermal imaging night sights. [Simon Watson]

38. The Mi-2 can also be fitted with a smoke generator. A tank containing chemicals is attached to the rear passenger compartment and the hot exhaust is blown through it via the large tubes visible in this photograph. Smoke is used as camouflage for tanks and troops on the battlefield as well as to hide vessels in their ports.

39. 'Black 347', an Mi-2 of the East German Air Force. This particular machine is painted in olive drab/earth brown on the upper surfaces and light blue underneath. The 'Winged Q' painted on the rear door is a symbol given to aircraft and helicopters in good condition, which have flown a certain number of hours without trouble. The first Mi-2s were delivered to East Germany in 1972, where they were used for pilot training as well as liaison and scouting duties. Another important duty was, until November 1989, the border patrol mission along the border with West Germany, and a considerable number of Mi-2s were therefore in service with the 'Grenztruppen der DDR' (Frontier Troops).

40. The Mi-2 can be armed with a flexible 7.62mm machine-gun on the starboard side (although the sight on this one is reminiscent of the First World War). The metal strip around the window edge is to protect the gunner from the airflow. Of interest is the flower pattern on the curtain of this Polish machine; a more functional curtain design for military versions was apparently not considered in Poland's Five-Year Plan.

41. The Mi-2 can also be equipped with two AT-3 'Sagger' anti-tank missiles on each side. The AT-3 is a wire-guided anti-tank missile with a range of between 550 and 3,200 metres. It remains in only very limited use in WarPac countries. A flexible 7.62mm gun is fitted in the rear window.

42. 'White 2128' an Mi-2 with a single Mars-2 pod for eight 57mm unguided missiles. A gunsight can be seen above the canopy containing the extinguisher on the starboard side, but in reality the 'Hoplite's' attack capabilities are limited; it has no armour protection and its large windows would be quite vulnerable to ground fire.

43. Three Yugoslav Mi-2s in a derelict state with rotors removed at Belgrade-Surcin airfield in late May 1989. All Mi-2s have been withdrawn from active service by the Yugoslav Air Force, which only operated a limited number. The Mi-2 nearest the camera has the full serial number 12514 applied in white on the tail boom, while the last three digits of the serial are repeated in white on the entrance door. All aircraft carry the early camouflage of dark green on the upper surfaces. [*Walter Hodel*]

44. The Ka-25 prototype was introduced to the public at the Tushino air display in 1961. Western sources erroneously allocated the designation Ka-20 to the helicopter and NATO dubbed the prototype 'Harp'. The Ka-25 prototype had a smaller search radar, more pointed rudders and no aft sliding rear door on the port side, compared with the standard production Ka-25. [*Robert Gretzyngier*]

45. Production of the Ka-25 started in 1966 and a year later the type was first observed by the West. This particular example of the 'Hormone-A' lacks the auxiliary fuel tanks on either side of the fuselage, which limits

its range to 400km. [*Robert Gretzyngier*]

46. A pair of Ka-25 'Hormone-As' without auxiliary fuel tanks landing on the deck of a '*Kiev*'-class aircraft-carrier. The first ship of this class, named *Kiev*, joined the Soviet Navy in 1975 and was followed by three more carriers, *Minsk*, *Novorossisk* and *Baku*. The later versions of the Ka-25 had uprated GTD-3BM turboshaft engines developing 990shp.

47. A pair of Mi-8TBs in their element as assault helicopters. Each can carry 28 fully equipped soldiers, as well as pods for unguided missiles. A Soviet assault regiment normally includes a single Mi-8 squadron and two Mi-24 squadrons. The 'Hip' is the most widely used helicopter in the world and undertakes transport duty in both military and civil service.

48. HS-4 is one of six Finnish Air Force Mi-8Ts. It arrived at Tampere Air Force Depot in 1974 in crates for assembly. The radar pod under the nose is unique to Finland. HS-4 is seen lifting a crankshaft from a Junkers Ju 88A-4 twin-engined bomber on its winch. Note the black kangaroo painted next to the flight insignia on the nose; this was applied by some visiting Australians. [*Hannu Valtonen*]

49. The Mi-8T is not a typical crane helicopter but can lift an underslung cargo of up to 3,000kg. The Mi-8 is therefore widely used in construction, and this Polish machine is being used on the railway network. The engineer on the ground is directing the pilot to the exact location, but in most cases there is a supervisor in radio-communication with the crew.

50. 'White 614', a Polish Mi-8TB, having its UB-16-57V pods loaded with S-5 unguided missiles. Once the missiles are in and the back of the pod is on, the weapon is ready to fire. The outrigger can be removed when not needed, on transport missions for instance. In addition to the pods (the UB-32-57V has now replaced the UB-16V), bombs can be carried on the pylons. The S-5 missile is of 57mm calibre, weighs 3.8kg and has a warhead of 800gm.

51. Soviet Mi-8TBs delivering troops during Exercise 'Druzba 86'. The casing under the tail boom houses the DIV-1 low speed precision airspeed indicator. On the bottom rear of the boom are the sender and receiver antennas of the RV-2 radioaltimeter. These particular 'Hip-Cs' have a light grey/light brown/olive drab camouflage on the upper surfaces. The tactical number 'Red 24' is outlined in white.

52. 'White 85', an Mi-8TB in the foreground, and Mi-17s in the background on the same exercise. By the mid-1980s, most 'Hips' had two- or three-tone camouflage, but 'White 85' is painted olive drab on the upper surfaces. Note the aerodynamic covering fitted above the hoist and the IRCM-jammer platform mounted on the rear of the engine covering, a rare feature on an Mi-8.

53. A flight of four East German Mi-8TBK 'Hip-Fs' during Exercise 'Waffen-brüderschaft 80' (Brothers in Arms), held in September 1980 in the German Democratic Republic. The 'Hips' have three pylons for weapons on each side, together with two AT-2 'Swatter' rails, and are equipped with a TBK-481 gun operated by the flight engineer. They are painted in light grey and olive drab on the upper surfaces, and light blue on the lower surfaces; the UB-32-57V pods are silver.

54. The fourth prototype Ka-26 'Hoodlum' carrying neither national markings nor registration. The two fins are of different dimensions and shape and there is a single large pitot tube fitted on the starboard side of the nose undercarriage. The main undercarriage is also slightly different from that of the standard Ka-26. [*Robert Gretzyngier*]

55. The Ka-26 does not operate with the East German Air Force but is in service with the Volkspolizei (People's Police). All have been modified with a loudspeaker on each side of the fuselage and a searchlight on the port side beside the nose wheel. [*Dr Volker Koos*]

56. Close-up of the co-axial rotor system of the Ka-26. This is a distinctive feature of all Kamov-built helicopters with the exception of the Ka-22 'Hoop'. The shafts are inclined forward by 6° and the main rotor blades are of glass-fibre, each of which weighs only 25kg. Rotor diameter on the Ka-26 is only 13.03m. [Dr Volker Koos]

57. Inside the cargo compartment of a Ka-26. The cabin can accommodate six passengers or two stretchers and is reached by two clamshell doors from the rear. The canopy is painted white inside and the door visible here leads to the pilot's compartment. [Dr Volker Koos]

58. 'Red 404', a Ka-26 of the Hungarian Air Force, the only WarPac country to use the type for military duties.

Initially designed for agricultural work, the Ka-26 was employed by the Hungarians in the scout and liaison role before it was replaced by the Mi-2 'Hoplite' and phased out in early 1988. [Tibor Sinka]

59. The successor to the Ka-26 is the Ka-126, which first flew on 19 October 1988 at the Kamov Hodynka test airfield near Moscow with G. Isajev at the controls. Instead of two radial engines, the Ka-126 is powered by a single gas turbine mounted on the fuselage behind the rotor. As a result the large covering for the engine is not needed. The Soviet Union handed over production of the type to the IAR State Aircraft Factory at Brasov in Romania, where several hundred Ka-126s are expected to be manufactured during the coming years.

58

59

60. The Mi-10 'Harke-A' flew for the first time in 1960. An unusual design feature is the 1° 30′ inclination of the fuselage, engines and main gearbox to starboard. This is to compensate for fuselage rotation as a result of the tail rotor thrust. The maximum load on the platform is 13,500kg and objects up to 3.75m high can be lifted. The Mi-10 was demonstrated to the West during the Paris Air Show. This picture was taken at Berlin-Schönefeld, Henschel's factory test field during the Second World War.

61. Mi-10 'Harke-A' SSSR-04102 at Warszawa-Okecie airport in Poland. The engine coverings are open to form a working platform for the ground crew. The Mi-10 has a crew of four, two pilots, a flight engineer and a radio operator. In a ground emergency the crew can escape from the cockpit by sliding down two cables which extend from the cabin roof. The Mi-10 has been exported to Iraq, Pakistan and the USA. Petroleum Helicopters purchased a single Mi-10 for use in oil exploration in Bolivia but the lack of spare parts for it from the USSR forced them to ground the 'Harke', which was subsequently scrapped.

62. The Mi-10K 'Harke-B' has a short-legged undercarriage and a cabin under the nose for the loadmaster who controls the load and directs the pilot. The Mi-10K has been used solely in the flying crane role, and is powered by two 6,500shp Soloviev D-25VF turboshaft engines. Many Mi-10Ks worked in Siberia building the oil pipelines. A group of 70 Mi-10Ks transported 45,000 tons of pipeline tubes and equipment to build the line between Samotlov and Kuibyshev. On some occasions the type carried one and a half times its maximum specified load (14,000kg). The Mi-10K was not exported outside the Soviet Union, but was used for similar work in other socialist countries.

63. The V-12 'Homer' was in its day the world's largest helicopter. It used the same configuration as the Ka-22 'Hoop' with engines fitted on its wingtips. It first flew on 18 June 1967, but the first flight only lasted 23 seconds. After several improvements, the helicopter flew again more than a year later and went on to capture a number of records, including taking a payload of 40,204kg to a height of 2,255m, a record that still stands. The V-12 had a length of 37.00m and a height of 12.50m. It used the same engines and rotor blades as the Mi-6, but it never entered production, hence the lack of the prefix 'Mi'.

64. Mi-24Ds and Mi-8TBKs take off for a training mission in May 1981. All the assault helicopters belong to Kampfhubschraubergeschwader 57 'Adolf von Lützow' based at Basephol. 'Black 417' (foreground) has only a single UB-32-57V pod fitted on the starboard inboard pylon; its camouflage is light grey and medium green on the upper and light blue on the lower surfaces.

65. The Izotov TV-3-117, two of which power the Mi-24, is a very reliable engine and has a much cooler exhaust than any Western helicopter. The camera is fitted only on the port wingtip of the 'Hind'. The stub wings help to unload the rotor at high speed and improve the helicopter's agility; they are also used for weapon stations.

66. A pilot boards his Mi-24D from the starboard side while the Weapons System Operator (WSO) enters through the port opening canopy. The rotor head is

made of titanum and the rotor blades are of fibre-glass skin, with an electrical de-icing system. Engine, rotor, tail rotor and gearbox are all very similar on the Mi-14, Mi-17 and Mi-24 and, to a certain degree, they are interchangeable.

67. A flight of three Polish Air Force Mi-24Ds shortly before take-off. Three Mi-24s are used in the armour hunting formation: two fly low ahead while the leader flies to the rear at a higher altitude. 'White 15' seen here was one of the first batch of 'Hinds' delivered to Poland in June 1979.

68. A Czech Air Force Mi-24D, 'White 0103'. At the time this picture was taken Czechoslovakia was believed to be the only WarPac country which had not changed the Cyrillic 'Opasno' (Danger) tail warning into its own language. This machine is camouflaged in light grey and medium green on the upper surfaces.

69. Ground crew arm an East German Mi-24D with AT-2 'Swatter' anti-tank missiles during a demonstration on 29 August 1985 at Holzdorf Air Base. This is the home of Jagdfliegerschwader 1 'Fritz Schmenkel'. The rotors are running and the pilot sits in his cockpit, while the WSO supervises the work of the ground crew. The front half of the AT-2 'Swatter' guidance pod is painted black, which is most unusual for a 'Hind-D.'

70. A Soviet Mi-24V 'Hind-E' in a low pass over the outskirts of Kabul, capital of Afghanistan. On each outboard pylon is an AT-6 'Spiral' anti-tank missile, but only a single pod for the 105mm missile is carried. The machine also carries three chaff/flare dispensers, installed above the national markings on each side, and an infra-red suppression box fitted on each side of the exhaust stubs which mix the hot exhaust with the cold air and blow them upwards into the downwash of the rotor.

71. 'White 1013', a Polish Mi-14PS, making a water landing in the Baltic. For such landings two flotation bags placed in the under-carriage fairing are inflated to give additional stability while on the water. The rotor, however, must continue to run to give additional stability. This Mi-14PS is painted light grey on the upper and light blue on the lower surfaces. The cross on the fuselage and the stripes on the tail boom are in red.

72. An Mi-14PS in the foreground with some Mi-14PLs behind. The main differences between the Mi-14PS (SAR variant) and the Mi-14PL (anti-submarine warfare) are that there is a large fairing on the Mi-14PS above the windows and a strake along the whole fuselage below the windows; there is also a small pod on the tail boom between the low-speed precision indicator and the tail; and on the nose there is a fairing housing the large searchlight. Both the Mi-14PS and Mi-14PL have a small retractable landing light in the nose.

73. This Mi-14BT 'Haze' was delivered to Libya where at least five are currently in service. It has light grey overall camouflage and a green dot for the national markings (green is the colour of Islam). To date, Mi-14s have been delivered to Bulgaria, Cuba, East Germany, Libya, Poland and Romania.

74

74. The Mi-14 'Haze' first flew in 1972 and production began in 1974. Three different versions are currently in service: Mi-14PL 'Haze-A' anti-submarine-warfare helicopter; Mi-14BT mine counter-measures variant; and Mi-14PS SAR variant (no ASCC name assigned to date). The Mi-14 is shore-based only, being too big for the 'Kiev'-class carriers. ASW Mi-14s always operate in pairs: one searches for and detects the enemy submarine and the other, weapon-carrying, machine attacks it.

75. A Soviet Navy Ka-29PL 'Helix-A' during an exercise in the Baltic. The 'Helix' was first observed by the West during Exercise 'Zapad 81', when spotted aboard the guided-missile destroyer *Udaloy*. The Ka-29 can fold its rotor and to date there are two different versions: the ASW Ka-29PL 'Helix-A' and the search and rescue Ka-29PS 'Helix-D'.

76. The Ka-29PS on which the civil Ka-32 is based. It has an external fuel tank on each side of the cabin and a winch next to the portside cabin door. The photograph shows an early experimental variant aboard a vessel and undergoing its operational trials.

77. The Mi-17TB was also supplied to the Sandanista government in Nicaragua where it saw extensive combat against the American-sponsored Contras. These 'Hip-Hs' were shipped in parts aboard a Soviet vessel and assembled in Nicaragua. The 'Hip-H' shown here is camouflaged light green and olive drab with light blue undersurfaces. The UB-32 pods are painted black.

75

76

77

78. This Soviet Air Force Mi-17TB is armed with six UB-32-57V pods and fitted with an IRCM jammer. The larger 80mm missile is now replacing the 57mm one seen here but, unlike the Mi-8TBK 'Hip-E/F', there is no provision to carry AT-2 'Swatter' missiles in pylons on top of the outriggers. [*Soldat und Technik via Günter Lippert*]

79. Soviet officers leaving an Mi-17TB. This machine has the blade-styled IFF antenna, which replaced the old three-pole 'Odd Rods' IFF from 1986 onwards on all IFF-equipped Soviet aircraft. The chaff/flare dispenser on the tail boom is fixed around it with straps. Differences between the Mi-17 and earlier Mi-8 include the upward fixed exhaust stubs and the rear-view mirror on the nose. A vortex/debris guard and a covering above the hoist are also fitted on later models of the Mi-8.

80. 'White 603', a Polish Mi-17TB, seen taking off in front of Warsaw's Central Station while operating in the flying crane role. This particular Mi-17TB lifted the motor and gear of the lift in a nearby skyscraper to the roof of the building. According to the pilots, the load carried by the 'Hip-H' was on the limit of its capacity.

81. Rear view of a Polish Mi-17TB; the main difference between the Mi-17 and Mi-8 is that the rail rotor has been moved to the port side. This particular machine is equipped with an IRCM jammer and a chaff/flare dispenser. The more powerful Izotov TV-117MT engine means that three instead of only two pylons can be carried as standard armament.

82. The Mi-17 'Hip-H' differs from the Mi-17 and Mi-8 in several respects. On this particular Czech 'Hip-H' the outriggers have been removed, but the different engine covering (with a tube for the APU's exhaust) contrasts it to the Mi-8. In addition, there is a large blister behind the exhaust stub, which is lacking on the Mi-8, while the small blister below the national marking has been repositioned on the Mi-8. [*Dusan Mikolas*]

83. Soviet soldiers return from a mission in Afghanistan. The Mi-17 is a very important transport vehicle linking the observation stations, built in unaccessible terrain around Kabul and elsewhere, with the main towns. The flying characteristics of the Mi-17 are much better than those of the Mi-24 'Hind', but the rate of

helicopter loss in combat due to enemy fire is much higher with the 'Hip'.

84. Czechoslovakia was the first WarPac country to receive the Mi-17. All the WarPac states are in deep financial trouble, making acquisition of new weaponry difficult; it should be noted that the Soviet Union wants

Western currency for a part of the price of such weapon exports. This Czech Mi-17, 'White 0803', is camouflaged in light grey and olive drab.

85. The Mi-26 can carry 20,000kg of freight over a distance of 800km at a cruising speed of 255km/h. The cockpit houses a crew of four, two pilots, a flight en-

gineer and navigator. The instrument panel has a TV monitor which the pilot uses to control the load in the cargo compartment with the help of a TV camera. [*Dusan Mikolas*]

86. The Mi-26 'Halo' has been introduced into the transport brigades of the Soviet Air Force. It can carry

about 100 infantrymen. This aircraft, 'Yellow 01', has the 'Excellent Aircraft' badge painted in red above the tactical number. The badge is given to aircraft and helicopters in good condition after accomplishing a required number of trouble-free flying hours. [*Soldat und Technik via Günter Lippert*]

87. This Mi-26 'Halo', 'Yellow 59', also has the 'Excellent Aircraft' badge, but this time in front of its tactical number. The Mi-26 first flew on 14 December 1977. It was designed to meet a requirement for a large transport helicopter to assist in the exploration of natural resources in Siberia and Central Asia. The Mi-26 is powered by two 11,400shp Lotarev D-136 engines coupled through a VR-26 gearbox. Dry weight of the D-136 is 1,050kg. [*Soldat und Technik via Günter Lippert*]

88. Maintenance on a Mi-26 'Halo' during a winter exercise. It is unarmed and has not been designed as a military troop carrier, but it can easily transport heavy vehicles such as the ZSU-23 AA-gun or the SA-9 SAM. It can also deliver a large quantity of ammunition and other supplies close to the front line, as no airfield is needed. [*Soldat und Technik via Günter Lippert*]

89. The very first 'Havoc', 'Yellow 012', which flew in November 1982. It has a different nose dome and chin-mounted electro-optics turret from those of the third prototype shown in the West. Note too the aerodynamic fairing over the cannon (which carries a sensor boom) and the shroud over the rear of the engine. Developed by Marat Tishchenko and M. V. Vaisberg, it offers the very latest in Soviet attack helicopter technology.